Du'ā

for

Beginners

اَلدُّعَاءُ سِلَاحُ الْمُؤْمِنِ

"Du'ā is the weapon of a believer."
(Mustadrak Hākim)

A concise and comprehensive collection of daily
Du'ās in the life of a Muslim

By
Shaykh Mufti Saiful Islām

© Copyright by JKN Publications

First Published in October 2010	5000 Copies
Second Edition, June 2012	3000 Copies
Third Edition, April 2014	5000 Copies
Fourth Edition, June 2016	5000 Copies
Fifth Edition, January 2019	5,000 Copies

ISBN 978-0-9565504-3-9

British Library Cataloguing in Publication Data
A catalogue record for this book is available from the British Library.

Publisher's Note:

Every care and attention has been put into the production of this book. If however, you find any errors they are our own, for which we seek Allāh's ﷻ forgiveness and reader's pardon.

Published by:

JKN Publications
118 Manningham Lane
Bradford
West Yorkshire
BD8 7JF
United Kingdom

t: +44 (0) 1274 308 456 | w: www.jkn.org.uk | e: info@jkn.org.uk

Book Title: Du'ā for Beginners

Author: Shaykh Mufti Saiful Islām

Printed by Mega Printing in Turkey

"In the Name of Allāh, the Most Beneficent,
the Most Merciful"

Contents

Introduction

بِسْمِ اللهِ الرَّحْمٰنِ الرَّحِيْمِ

All praise belongs to Allāh 🕮. We praise Him, seek His assistance alone and beseech forgiveness from Him. We seek refuge in Allāh 🕮 from the evil of our souls and from our evil deeds. Indeed, who-ever Allāh 🕮 guides, none can misguide and whoever He mis-guides, there is none that can guide him. I bear witness and testify that there is no god worthy of worship except Allāh 🕮, all glory be to Him and I bear witness and testify that Prophet Muhammad 🕮 is His final Messenger and His perfect worshipper.

Verily, man has been created for a noble and great purpose. The most noble and dignified objective that exists in a believer is that he worships Allāh 🕮 alone, without associating any partners unto Him.

Allāh 🕮 states in the Holy Qur'ān:

وَمَا خَلَقْتُ الْجِنَّ وَالْاِنْسَ اِلَّا لِيَعْبُدُوْنِ

"And I have only created jinn and mankind to worship Me." (51:56)

Amongst the greatest and most noble form of worship is Du'ā (supplication). It is a plea from the very heart of a believer directed towards Allāh 🕮, the Hearer of all things, the Knower of all secrets.

It is a confession that emanates from the heart of a believer that he is weak, feeble and helpless who cannot achieve anything without Allāh's ﷻ help and support.

The Holy Prophet ﷺ has said:

اَلدُّعَاءُ مُخُّ الْعِبَادَةِ

"Du'ā is the essence of worship." (Tirmizi)

Du'ā has been called the essence of worship for two main reasons. First by supplicating to Allāh ﷻ, a person fulfils his obligation of invoking unto Allāh ﷻ, which is understood from the verse:

وَقَالَ رَبُّكُمُ ادْعُوْنِيْ اَسْتَجِبْ لَكُمْ

"And your Lord says, 'Call Me, I will answer you (your prayer)'." (40:60)

This is worship in its purest form. Second, by asking Allāh ﷻ, one realises that only He can fulfil one's needs. The servant who calls upon his Lord abandons hope in everything else and turns his full attention towards Allāh ﷻ, humbling himself in front of Him. This is the essence of worship.

So with the noble status of this act of worship in mind, I have compiled this short, but comprehensive book for our Muslim brothers and sisters especially our young children who are studying in their local Makātib and Islamic institutes in the U.K and abroad.

The treatise has been titled, "Du'ā for Beginners" which contains basic Du'ās which every Muslim should recite on a daily basis. It is my earnest hope that this book will be introduced to our beloved young children in Islamic schools and Madrasahs so that they can cherish this beautiful treasure of supplications of our beloved Prophet ﷺ in their daily lives, which will ultimately bring peace and happiness in both worlds, Inshā-Allāh.

May Allāh ﷻ accept this humble effort and make it a means of our salvation in the Hereafter. Āmīn.

(Shaykh Mufti) Saiful Islām
Chief Editor, Al-Mu'min Magazine
Principal, Jāmiah Khātamun Nabiyeen, Bradford, UK
Dhul-Qa'dah 1431/October 2010

The Excellence of Du'ā

Du'ā is the most noble act in the sight of Allāh ﷻ. Sayyidunā Abū Hurairah ؓ relates that the Holy Prophet ﷺ said:

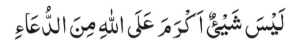

"There is nothing that is more noble in the sight of Allāh ﷻ than Du'ā." (Tirmizi, Ibn Mājah)

Some Benefits of Du'ā

1. Du'ā is the best act of worship.
2. Du'ā is the essence of worship.
3. Du'ā is a sign of one's Imān.
4. To make Du'ā is obeying Allāh ﷻ.
5. Allāh ﷻ is close to the one making Du'ā.
6. Du'ā is a sign of humility.
7. Du'ā cools Allāh's ﷻ anger.
8. Du'ā is a cause of being saved from the Fire of Hell.
9. The reward of Du'ā is guaranteed.
10. Du'ā is a cure for all diseases.

Ādāb (etiquettes) of Du'ā

When supplicating to Allāh ﷻ, the following etiquettes should be observed:

1. Abstain from Harām (unlawful) food, drink and clothing.
2. Abstain from an unlawful income.
3. Be sincere in what you ask for.
4. Attempt to perform a good deed before making Du'ā.
5. Confess to one's sins.
6. Be in the state of Wudhu.
7. Face the Qiblah.
8. Sit in the Qa'idah position.
9. Praise Allāh ﷻ before and after the Du'ā.
10. Send Durūd upon the Holy Prophet ﷺ.
11. Make Du'ā through the mediation of Allāh's ﷻ beautiful names.
12. Recite Du'ās mentioned in the various Ahādīth, for the Holy Prophet ﷺ did not leave out any aspect of human need for which he did not make Du'ā.
13. Begin by first making Du'ā for oneself, then for one's parents, family then for the whole Ummah.
14. After completing the Du'ā, pass your hands over your face.
15. Do not ask for anything that involves sins, for instance, the breaking of relations etc.
16. Do not be impatient, expecting the Du'ā to be granted immediately.
17. Make Du'ā with conviction regarding its acceptance.

18.   The Du'ā should be made from the depth of the heart and with full devotion, for Allāh ﷻ does not accept the Du'ā of a careless person.

Note: All the abovementioned etiquettes of Du'ā have been proven from the Ahādīth.

Moments in which Du'ās are accepted

1.   While the Adhān is in progress. (Abū Dāwūd)
2.   The period between the Adhān and the Iqāmat. (Abū Dāwūd, Tirmizi, Nasai)
3.   After the Fardh Salāh. (Tirmizi, Nasai)
4.   After the recitation of the Holy Qur'ān. (Tirmizi)
5.   After completion of the Holy Qur'ān. (Tabarāni)
6.   While drinking the water of Zam Zam. (Mustadrak)
7.   When there is a gathering of many Muslims. (Sihāh-Sitta - the six authentic books of Ahādīth)
8.   When it rains. (Abū Dāwūd)
9.   Whenever a person sees the Ka'bah. (Tirmizi)
10.   In the gathering of Dhikr. (Bukhāri,Muslim, Tirmizi)

Special moments in which Du'ās are accepted

1.   On the night of Qadr (Laylatul-Qadr). (Tirmizi, Nasai)
2.   On the day of Arafah. (Tirmizi)
3.   During the month of Ramadhān. (Bazzār)
4.   On the eve of Friday (the night preceding Friday). (Tirmizi)

11

5.   During the entire day of Friday. (Abū Dāwūd, Nasai)
6.   During the final portion of the night. (Musnad Ahmad)
7.   At the time of Suhūr. (Musnad Ahmad)
8.   On Friday during the Jumuah Salāh, from the time the Imām
     sits on the Mimbar (pulpit) until the end of Jumuāh Salāh.

                                                        (Muslim)

Places where Duā's are accepted

It is hoped that Du'as will be accepted at all those Islamic sites and places that are regarded as sacred. Sayyidunā Hasan Basri ۞ once wrote a letter to the people of Makkah stating those sacred places where there is hope of Du'ā being accepted. They are as follows:

1.   At the blessed grave of the Holy Prophet ۞.
2.   Matāf (circuit) in which the Tawāf of Ka'bah takes place.
3.   Multazam - the area between Al-Hajarul-Aswad (Black stone)
     and the door of the Ka'bah.
4.   Under the Mīzāb (water spout) of the Ka'bah.
5.   Inside the Ka'bah.
6.   At the well of Zam Zam.
7.   On the mounts of Safā and Marwa.
8.   In the area where pilgrims walk between Safā and Marwa.
9.   Behind Maqām Ibrāhīm (the stone containing the footprint of
     Sayyidunā Ibrāhīm ۞).
10. In the plain of Arafah.
11. In Muzdalifah.
12. In Minā.
13. At the Jamarāt (stone pillars) where the Shayātīn are pelted.

Those people whose Du'ās are accepted

1. A poor person and the one who is in dire need.(Bukhāri, Muslim)
2. An oppressed person, even if he is a non-believer or sinful. (Musnad Ahmad)
3. Parent's Du'ā for their children. (Abū Dāwūd, Tirmizi)
4. The Du'ā of a just king or ruler. (Ibn Mājah, Tirmizi)
5. The Du'ā of a righteous person. (Bukhāri, Muslim)
6. Du'ā of children who are kind and obedient to their parents. (Muslim)
7. Du'ā of the traveller. (Abū Dāwūd, Ibn Mājah)
8. The Du'ā of a fasting person at the time of breaking the fast. (Tirmizī, Ibn Mājah)
9. A Muslim's Du'ā for another in his or her absence. (Muslim, Abū Dāwūd)
10. The pilgrim's Du'ā until he or she returns home.(Jāmi Abū Mansūr)

Everyday Du'ās in the Life of a Muslim

1. At the time of sleeping

اَللّٰهُمَّ بِاسْمِكَ اَمُوتُ وَ اَحْيٰ

[Allāhumma bismika amūtu wa ahyā]

"O Allāh, by Your Name I die and I live."
(Bukhārī, Muslim)

2. Upon waking up

اَلْحَمْدُ لِلّٰهِ الَّذِىْ اَحْيَانَا بَعْدَ مَا
اَمَاتَنَا وَاِلَيْهِ النُّشُوْرُ

[Al-hamdu-lil-lāhil-ladhī ahyānā ba'da mā amātanā
wa ilayhin-nushūr]

**"Praise be to Allāh Who gave us life after having given us
death and to Him is (our) final return."** (Bukhārī)

3. When entering the toilet

$$اَللّٰهُمَّ اِنِّيْ اَعُوْذُ بِكَ مِنَ الْخُبُثِ وَالْخَبَآئِثِ$$

[Allāhumma inni a'ūdhu-bika minal-khubuthi wal-khabāith]

"O Allāh I seek Your protection from male and female demons." (Bukhāri, Muslim)

4. After leaving the toilet

$$غُفْرَانَكَ اَلْحَمْدُ لِلّٰهِ الَّذِيْ اَذْهَبَ$$
$$عَنِّى اُلاَذٰى وَعَافَانِيْ$$

[Ghufrānaka Alhamdu-lil-lāhil-ladhī adhaba annil'adhā wa-ā-fāni]

"O Allāh, I seek Your forgiveness, praise be to Allāh Who relieved me of discomfort and granted me comfort." (Ibn Mājah)

15

5. Before beginning Wudhu (ablution)

When sitting to perform Wudhu, first of all read Bismillāh. Thereafter, read the following Du'ā:

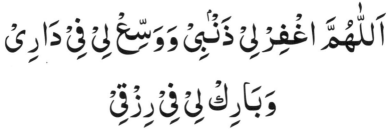

[Allāhummagfir-lī-dhambī-wa- wassi-lī-fī-dārī-
wa-bārik-lī-fī-rizqī]

"O Allāh, forgive my sins, make spacious my home and bless my sustenance." (Ibnus-Sunni)

6. After completing Wudhu

أَشْهَدُ أَنْ لَّا إِلٰهَ إِلَّا اللهُ وَحْدَهُ

لَا شَرِيْكَ لَهُ وَأَشْهَدُ اَنَّ مُحَمَّدًا عَبْدُهُ وَرَسُوْلُهُ

[Ash-hadu-allā-ilāha-illal-lāhu-wahdahū-lā-sharīka-lahū wa-
ash-hadu anna-Muhammadan-abduhū-wa-Rasūluh]

"I bear witness that there is no god but Allāh, He is One and has no partner and I bear witness that Muhammad is His Servant and Messenger."

"Whoever recites this Du'ā, the eight doors of Paradise will be opened for him." (Muslim, Abū Dāwūd)

Thereafter, recite the following Du'ā:

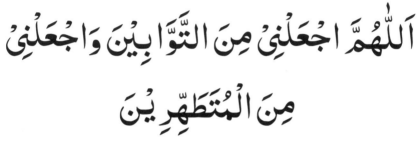

[Allāhummaj-alnī minat-tawābīna-waj-alnī-minal-muta-tahhirīn]

"O Allāh, make me of those who repent and of those who maintain purity."
(Tirmizi)

7. After hearing the Adhān (the call to Salāh)

اَللّٰهُمَّ رَبَّ هٰذِهِ الدَّعْوَةِ التَّآمَّةِ وَالصَّلَاةِ
الْقَآئِمَةِ اٰتِ مُحَمَّدَا إِ الْوَسِيلَةَ وَالْفَضِيلَةَ
وَابْعَثْهُ مَقَامًا مَّحْمُوْدَا إِ الَّذِي وَعَدْتَّهُ

[Allāhumma- rabba-hādhihi'd-da'wati't-tāmmati-was- salātil-
qā'ima (ti), āti-muhammadanil-wasīlata-walfadhila (ta),
wab'ath-hu-maqāmam-mahmūdanil- ladhī-wa'attah]

**"O Allāh, Lord of this perfect call and established Salāh,
grant Muhammad a place near to You, an excellence and exalted degree, and raise him to the praiseworthy station that
You have promised him."**

"Whoever recites this Du'ā will gain the intercession of the
Holy Prophet ﷺ on the Day of Judgement."(Bukhāri)

18

8. When entering the Masjid

When entering the Masjid, a person should send Durūd upon the Holy Prophet ﷺ and thereafter recite the following Du'ā:

[Allāhummaf-taḥlī-abwāba rahmatik]

"O Allāh, open for me the doors of Your mercy."
(Muslim, Abū Dāwūd)

9. When leaving the Masjid

[Allāhumma-innī-as'aluka-min-fadhlik]

"O Allāh, I ask of You Your favour."
(Muslim, Abū Dāwūd)

19

10. Before eating

بِسْمِ اللهِ وَبَرَكَةِ اللهِ

[Bismillāhi-wa-barakatillāh]

"In the name of Allāh and with the blessing of Allāh." (Mustadrak Hākim)

11. After eating

اَلْحَمْدُ لِلهِ الَّذِىٓ أَطْعَمَنَا وَسَقَانَا
وَجَعَلَنَا مُسْلِمِيْنَ

[Alhamdu-lil-lāhil-ladhī-at'amanā-wa-saqāna-waja alanā muslimīn]

"Praise be to Allāh Who fed us and gave us to drink and made us Muslims."
(Abū Dāwūd)

12. When forgetting to recite the Du'ā before eating, then upon remembering one should recite:

بِسْمِ اللهِ اَوَّلَهُ وَاخِرَهُ

[Bismillāhi-awwalahu-wa-ākhirah]

"In the name of Allāh, at the beginning of it (the meal) and at the end of it."
(Abū Dāwūd)

13. At the time of completing the fast:

اَللّٰهُمَّ لَكَ صُمْتُ وَعَلٰى رِزْقِكَ اَفْطَرْتُ

[Allāhumma-laka-sumtu-wa'alā-rizqi-ka-aftartu]

"O Allāh for You I have fasted and by what (food) You have blessed me with, have I broken it."
(Abū Dāwūd in his Marāsil)

14. When eating at someone's house or after eating food by invitation

اَللّٰهُمَّ اَطْعِمْ مَنْ اَطْعَمَنِیْ وَاسْقِ مَنْ سَقَانِیْ

[Allāhumma-at'im-man-at'amanī-wasqi-man- saqānī]

"O Allāh feed those who have fed me and give drink to those who have given me drink."
(Muslim)

15. After drinking milk

اَللّٰهُمَّ بَارِكْ لَنَا فِيْهِ وَزِدْنَا مِنْهُ

[Allāhumma-bārik-lanā-fīhi-wa-zidnā-minhu]

"O Allāh, bless us in it and increase us by it."
(Tirmizi)

16. When drinking Zam Zam water

اَللّٰهُمَّ اِنِّىْ اَسْـَٔلُكَ عِلْمًا نَّافِعًا وَّرِزْقًا وَّاسِعًا
وَّشِفَآءً مِّنْ كُلِّ دَآءٍ

[Allāhumma-innī-as'aluka-ilman-nāfi-aw-wa-rizqaw
wāsi-aw-wa-shifā'am-min-kulli-dā-in]

**"O Allāh, I ask of You (to give me) beneficial knowledge,
ample provisions and restoration from every illness."**
(Mustadrak Hākim)

17. When putting on clothing

اَلْحَمْدُ لِلّٰهِ الَّذِىْ كَسَانِىْ هٰذَا وَرَزَقَنِيْهِ
مِنْ غَيْرِ حَوْلٍ مِّنِّىْ وَلَا قُوَّةٍ

[Alhamdu-lillāhil-ladhī-kasāni-hādhā-warazaqanīhi-min-
ghayri-hawlim-minnī-walā-quwwatin]

"Praise be to Allāh Who clothed me in this and gave it to me without any strength and ability on my part."

"Whoever recites this Du'ā, his past and present sins will be forgiven." (Abū Dāwūd, Tirmizi)

18. When putting on new clothing

$$اَلْحَمْدُ لِلّٰهِ الَّذِىْ كَسَانِىْ مَا أُوَارِىْ بِهٖ عَوْرَتِىْ$$

$$وَ اَتَجَمَّلُ بِهٖ فِىْ حَيَاتِىْ$$

[Alhamdu-lillāhil-ladhī-kasānī-ma-uwāri-bihī-awratī-wa-ata-jammalu-bihī-fī-hayātī]

"Praise be to Allāh Who clothed me
with what covers my nakedness and with that by which I
adorn myself in my life."
(Tirmizi, Ibn Mājah)

19. When leaving the home

بِسْمِ اللهِ تَوَكَّلْتُ عَلَى اللهِ لَا حَوْلَ

وَلَا قُوَّةَ اِلَّا بِاللهِ

[Bismillāhi-tawakkaltu-alal-lāhi-lā-hawla-walā
quwwata-illā-billāh]

**"In the name of Allāh, I depend on Allāh, and there is no
power (to do good) nor restraint (to avoid evil)
except with Allāh."**

When anyone reads this Du'ā, the Angels say to him, "You
have been guided and have been saved (from all harms)."
(Abū Dāwūd, Tirmizi)

20. When entering the home

اَللّٰهُمَّ اِنِّیْ اَسْاَلُكَ خَیْرَ الْمَوْلَجِ وَخَیْرَ الْمَخْرَجِ بِسْمِ

اللهِ وَلَجْنَا وَبِسْمِ اللهِ خَرَجْنَا وَعَلَی اللهِ رَبِّنَا تَوَکَّلْنَا

[Allāhumma-innī-as'aluka-khayral-mawlaji-wa-khayral-
makhraji-bismillāhi-walajnā-wa-bismillāhi kharajnā-wa-alal-
lāhi-rabbinā-tawakkalnā]

"O Allāh I beseech You the blessing of entering and
leaving. In Allāh's name we enter and in Allāh's name we
leave and in Allāh, our Lord, we trust ."
(Abū Dāwūd)

21. When looking in the mirror

[Allāhumma-ahsanta-khalqī fahassin-khuluqī]

"O Allāh! You made my external appearance good,
so make me good in morals (too)."
(Ahmad)

22. When greeting someone

اَلسَّلَامُ عَلَيْكُمْ وَرَحْمَةُ اللهِ وَبَرَكَاتُهُ

[Assalāmu-alaykum-wa-rahmatullāhi-wa-barakātuh]

"May peace be upon you and the mercy of Allāh and His blessings."

When replying to the greeting of anyone's Salām, then say the following:

وَعَلَيْكُمُ السَّلَامُ وَرَحْمَةُ اللهِ وَبَرَكَاتُهُ

[Wa-alaykumus-salām-wa-rahmatullāhi-wa-barakātuh]

**"May peace be upon you also
and the mercy of Allāh and His blessings."**
(Abū Dāwūd, Tirmizi)

Note:
When one receives the Salām of anyone by means of another person, then say the following:

عَلَيْكَ وَعَلَيْهِ السَّلَامُ وَرَحْمَةُ اللهِ وَبَرَكَاتُهُ

[Alaika wa-alayhis-salām-wa-rahmatullāhi-wa-barakātuh]

(Hisn Hasīn)

23. When bidding someone farewell

اَسْتَوْدِعُ اللهَ دِيْنَكَ وَاَمَانَتَكَ وَخَوَاتِيْمَ عَمَلِكَ

[Astawdi-ul-lāha-dīnaka-wa-amānataka-wa-khawātīma-amalika]

**"I entrust Allāh with your religion, your belongings
and the result of your deeds."**
(Tirmizi)

24. When boarding a vehicle or mounting an animal

While boarding or mounting recite first:

بِسْمِ اللهِ

[Bismillāh]

"In the name of Allāh."

When comfortably seated and ready to go then recite:

[Alhamdu-lillāh]

"Praise be to Allāh."

Thereafter recite:

سُبْحَانَ الَّذِیْ سَخَّرَ لَنَا هٰذَا وَمَا كُنَّا لَهٗ

مُقْرِنِیْنَ وَاِنَّا اِلٰی رَبِّنَا لَمُنْقَلِبُوْنَ

[Subhānalladhī-sakkhara-lanā-hādhā-wamā-kunnā lahū-
muqrinīna-wa-innā-ilā-rabbinā-la-munqalibūn]

**"Exalted is He Who subdued this to us, and we could not
have subdued it, verily to our Lord we return." (43:13)**

Thereafter recite thrice:

اَلْحَمْدُ لِلّٰهِ

[Alhamdu-lillāh]

"**Praise be to Allāh.**"
Then recite thrice:

اَللّٰهُ اَكْبَرُ

[Allāhu-akbar]

"**Allāh is the greatest.**"

Recite the following Du'ā for Istighfār (forgiveness):

سُبْحَانَكَ اِنِّیْ ظَلَمْتُ نَفْسِیْ فَاغْفِرْ لِیْ فَاِنَّهٗ

لَا يَغْفِرُ الذُّنُوْبَ اِلَّا اَنْتَ

[Subhānaka-innī-zalamtu-nafsī-faghfirlī-fa-innahū-lā- yagh-
firuz-zunūba-illā-anta]

"**Exalted are You (O Allāh) verily I have wronged myself,
so forgive me as none but You forgive sins.**"
(Abū Dāwūd, Tirmizi)

25. When returning home from a journey

اَئِبُوْنَ تَائِبُوْنَ عَابِدُوْنَ لِرَبِّنَا حَامِدُوْنَ

[Ā-ibūna-tā-ibūna-ābidūna-lirabbinā-hāmidūn]

**"We now return (from our journey) repenting (to Allāh),
worshipping (Him) and praising our Lord (Allāh)."**
(Bukhārī, Muslim)

26. When sneezing

[Alhamdu-lillāh]

"Praise be to Allāh."

One who hears should respond by saying:

[Yar-hamu-kallāh]
"Allāh's mercy be upon you."

Then the one who sneezed, upon hearing the response
should say:

يَهْدِيْكُمُ اللهُ وَيُصْلِحُ بَالَكُمْ

[Yahdī-kumullāhu-wa-yuslihu-bālakum]

"May Allāh guide you and rectify your condition."
(Bukhāri)

27. When thanking someone

جَزَاكَ اللهُ خَيْرًا

[Jazāk-Allāhu-khayran]

"May Allāh reward you well."
(Tirmizi, Nasai)

28. When seeing a Muslim happy

[Adhakallāhu-sinnak]

"May Allāh fill your life with laughter."
(Bukhāri, Abū Dāwūd)

29. When entering a market or shopping centre

لَا اِلٰهَ اِلَّا اللّٰهُ وَحْدَهُ لَا شَرِيْكَ لَهُ لَهُ الْمُلْكُ وَلَهُ الْحَمْدُ يُحْيِىْ وَيُمِيْتُ وَهُوَ حَيٌّ لَا يَمُوْتُ بِيَدِهِ الْخَيْرُ وَهُوَ عَلٰى كُلِّ شَيْءٍ قَدِيْرٌ

[Lā-ilāha-illallāhu-wahdahu-lā-sharīka-lahu, lahul- mulku-walahul-hamdu, yuhyī-wa-yumīt, wahuwa- hayyul-lā-yamūtu, biyadihil-khayr, wahuwa-alā-kulli- shay'in-qadīr]

"There is no god but Allāh, He is One and has no partner. His is the kingdom and to Him is all praise. He gives life and gives death; He is living, not subject to death. In His Hand is goodness and He has power over all things."

Whoever recites this Du'ā, Allāh ﷻ will reward him with one million good deeds, forgive one million of his sins, and raise his rank by one million degrees. (Tirmizi, Mustadrak Hākim)

30. When seeing a fire

[Allāhu-akbar]

"Allāh is the greatest." (Ibnus-Sunni)

31. When hearing the barking of a dog or the braying of a donkey

اَعُوْذُ بِاللهِ مِنَ الشَّيْطَانِ الرَّجِيْمِ

[A'ūdhu-billāhi-minashaytānir-rajīm]

"I seek refuge in Allāh from Shaytān, the accursed."
(Abū Dāwūd)

32. When afraid of a person, group or nation

مِنْ شُرُوْرِهِمْ

[Allāhumma-innā-naj'aluka-fī-nuhū-rihim-wa-na-'ūdhu-bika-
min-shurūrihim]

**"O Allāh, we place You before them and seek Your protec-
tion against their mischief."** (Abū Dāwūd)

33. When feeling pain in the body

Place the right hand on the affected area and recite Bismillāh
three times and thereafter recite the following Du'ā seven
times:

اَعُوْذُ بِعِزَّةِ اللهِ وَقُدْرَتِهِ مِنْ شَرِّ مَا اَجِدُ وَاُحَاذِرُ

[A'ūdhu-bi'izzatil-lāhi-wa-qudratihī-min-sharri-mā- ajidu
wa-uhādhir]

**"I seek refuge in the might and power of Allāh,
from the evil of the pain I feel and fear."**
(Muslim, Muwatta Mālik)

34. When feeling helpless regarding a matter:

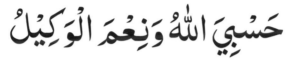

[Hasbiyallāhu-wa-ni'mal-wakīl]

"Allāh is my sufficiency, and how perfect a Benefactor (is He)." (Abū Dāwūd)

35. When one becomes angry:

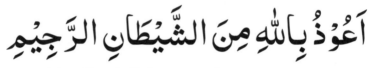

[A'ūdhu-billāhi-minashaytānir-rajīm]

"I seek refuge in Allāh from Shaytān, the accursed."
(Bukhāri, Muslim)

36. When Shaytān places doubts regarding one's faith

اَعُوْذُ بِاللهِ مِنَ الشَّيْطَانِ الرَّجِيْمِ اٰمَنْتُ بِاللهِ

[A'ūdhu-billāhi-minashaytānir-rajīm - Āmantu-billāh]

**"I seek refuge in Allāh from Shaytān, the accursed.
I believe in Allāh."** (Muslim)

37. When afflicted by any illness or disease:

اَللّٰهُمَّ رَبَّ النَّاسِ اَذْهِبِ الْبَأْسَ اِشْفِ
اَنْتَ الشَّافِيْ لَا شِفَاءَ اِلَّا شِفَاؤُكَ شِفَاءٌ
لَا يُغَادِرُ سَقَمًا

[Allāhumma-rabban-nāsi adh-hibil'ba'sa-ishfi-antash- shāfī-lā
-shifā'a-illā-shifā-uka shifā'ul-lā-yughādiru- saqaman]

**"O Allāh, Lord of mankind, remove all harm, cure as You
are the One Who cures. There is no cure but Your cure. A
cure that leaves no illness."** (Bukhārī, Muslim)

38. When visiting a person who is ill

لَا بَأْسَ طَهُوْرٌ اِنْ شَآءَ اللهُ

[Lā-ba'sa-tahūrun-In-shā–Allāh]

"No need to worry. It (this illness) is a purifier (of sins), Allāh willing." (Bukhāri)

39. Prayer for the morning and evening (for protection from all evils)

بِسْمِ اللهِ الَّذِیْ لَا یَضُرُّ مَعَ اسْمِهِ شَیْءٌ فِی الْاَرْضِ وَلَا فِی السَّمَآءِ وَهُوَ السَّمِیْعُ الْعَلِیْمُ

[Bismillāhil-ladhī-lā-yadhurru-ma'asmihī-shay'un-fil-ardhi-walā-fis-samā'i-wahuwas-samī-ul-alīm]

"In the name of Allāh by Whose name nothing on earth and nothing in heaven can cause harm, He is All-Hearing, All-Knowing."

Whoever reads this Du'ā thrice in the morning or evening, nothing will harm him till the night or morning. (Tirmizi)

40. At the end of a gathering (of sacred knowledge or religious discussion)

سُبْحَانَكَ اللّٰهُمَّ وَبِحَمْدِكَ اَشْهَدُ اَنْ لَّا اِلٰهَ

اِلَّا اَنْتَ اَسْتَغْفِرُكَ وَاَتُوْبُ اِلَيْكَ

[Subhānaka-Allāhumma-wabihamdika-ash-hadu-allā- ilāha-illā-anta astaghfiruka-wa-atūbu-ilayk]

"Exalted are You O Allāh, by Your praise: I bear witness that there is no god but You. I seek forgiveness from You and I repent to You."

Whoever recites this Du'ā will have all the sins committed by him in the gathering forgiven. (Tirmizi)

Some of the Titles from JKN PUBLICATIONS

Your Questions Answered

An outstanding book written by Shaykh Mufti Saiful Islām. A very comprehensive yet simple Fatāwa book and a source of guidance that reaches out to a wider audience i.e. the English speaking Muslims. The reader will benefit from the various answers to questions based on the Laws of Islām relating to the beliefs of Islām, knowledge, Sunnah, pillars of Islām, marriage, divorce and contemporary issues.

UK RRP: £7.50

Hadeeth for Beginners

A concise Hadeeth book with various Ahādīth that relate to basic Ibādāh and moral etiquettes in Islām accessible to a wider readership. Each Hadeeth has been presented with the Arabic text, its translation and commentary to enlighten the reader, its meaning and application in day-to-day life.

UK RRP: £3.00

Du'ā for Beginners

This book contains basic Du'ās which every Muslim should recite on a daily basis. Highly recommended to young children and adults studying at Islamic schools and Madrasahs so that one may cherish the beautiful treasure of supplications of our beloved Prophet 🕌 in one's daily life, which will ultimately bring peace and happiness in both worlds, Inshā-Allāh.

UK RRP: £2.00

How well do you know Islām?

An exciting educational book which contains 300 multiple questions and answers to help you increase your knowledge on Islām! Ideal for the whole family, especially children and adult students to learn new knowledge in an enjoyable way and cherish the treasures of knowledge that you will acquire from this book. A very beneficial tool for educational syllabus.

UK RRP: £3.00

Treasures of the Holy Qur'ān

This book entitled "Treasures of the Holy Qur'ān" has been compiled to create a stronger bond between the Holy Qur'ān and the readers. It mentions the different virtues of Sūrahs and verses from the Holy Qur'ān with the hope that the readers will increase their zeal and enthusiasm to recite and inculcate the teachings of the Holy Qur'ān into their daily lives.

UK RRP: £3.00

Some of the Titles from JKN PUBLICATIONS

Marriage - A Complete Solution

Islām regards marriage as a great act of worship. This book has been designed to provide the fundamental teachings and guidelines of all what relates to the marital life in a simplified English language. It encapsulates in a nutshell all the marriage laws mentioned in many of the main reference books in order to facilitate their understanding and implementation.

UK RRP: £5.00

Pearls of Luqmān

This book is a comprehensive commentary of Sūrah Luqmān, written beautifully by Shaykh Mufti Saiful Islām. It offers the reader with an enquiring mind, abundance of advice, guidance, counselling and wisdom.

The reader will be enlightened by many wonderful topics and anecdotes mentioned in this book, which will create a greater understanding of the Holy Qur'ān and its wisdom. The book highlights some of the wise sayings and words of advice Luqmān ﷺ gave to his son.

UK RRP: £3.00

Arabic Grammar For Beginners

This book is a study of Arabic Grammar based on the subject of Nahw (Syntax) in a simplified English format. If a student studies this book thoroughly, he/she will develop a very good foundation in this field, Inshā-Allāh. Many books have been written on this subject in various languages such as Arabic, Persian and Urdu. However, in this day and age there is a growing demand for this subject to be available in English .

UK RRP: £3.00

A Gift to My Youngsters

This treasure filled book, is a collection of Islamic stories, morals and anecdotes from the life of our beloved Prophet ﷺ, his Companions ﷺ and the pious predecessors. The stories and anecdotes are based on moral and ethical values, which the reader will enjoy sharing with their peers, friends, families and loved ones.

"A Gift to My Youngsters" – is a wonderful gift presented to the readers personally by the author himself, especially with the youngsters in mind. He has carefully selected stories and anecdotes containing beautiful morals, lessons and valuable knowledge and wisdom.

UK RRP: £5.00

Travel Companion

The beauty of this book is that it enables a person on any journey, small or distant or simply at home, to utilise their spare time to read and benefit from an exciting and vast collection of important and interesting Islamic topics and lessons. Written in simple and easy to read text, this book will immensely benefit both the newly interested person in Islām and the inquiring mind of a student expanding upon their existing knowledge. Inspiring reminders from the Holy Qur'ān and the blessed words of our beloved Prophet ﷺ beautifies each topic and will illuminate the heart of the reader. **UK RRP: £5.00**

Pearls of Wisdom

Junaid Baghdādi ﷺ once said, "Allāh ﷻ strengthens through these Islamic stories the hearts of His friends, as proven from the Qur'anic verse,
"And all that We narrate unto you of the stories of the Messengers, so as to strengthen through it your heart." (11:120)
Mālik Ibn Dinār ﷺ stated that such stories are gifts from Paradise. He also emphasised to narrate these stories as much as possible as they are gems and it is possible that an individual might find a truly rare and invaluable gem among them. **UK RRP: £6.00**

Inspirations

This book contains a compilation of selected speeches delivered by Shaykh Mufti Saiful Islām on a variety of topics such as the Holy Qur'ān, Nikāh and eating Halāl. Having previously been compiled in separate booklets, it was decided that the transcripts be gathered together in one book for the benefit of the reader. In addition to this, we have included in this book, further speeches which have not yet been printed.

UK RRP: £6.00

Gift to my Sisters

A thought provoking compilation of very interesting articles including real life stories of pious predecessors, imaginative illustrations and much more. All designed to influence and motivate mothers, sisters, wives and daughters towards an ideal Islamic lifestyle. A lifestyle referred to by our Creator, Allāh ﷻ in the Holy Qur'ān as the means to salvation and ultimate success. **UK RRP: £6.00**

Gift to my Brothers

A thought provoking compilation of very interesting articles including real life stories of pious predecessors, imaginative illustrations, medical advices on intoxicants and rehabilitation and much more. All designed to influence and motivate fathers, brothers, husbands and sons towards an ideal Islamic lifestyle. A lifestyle referred to by our Creator, Allāh ﷻ in the Holy Qur'ān as the means to salvation and ultimate success.

UK RRP: £5.00

Heroes of Islām

"In the narratives there is certainly a lesson for people of intelligence (understanding)." (12:111)

A fine blend of Islamic personalities who have been recognised for leaving a lasting mark in the hearts and minds of people.

A distinguishing feature of this book is that the author has selected not only some of the most world and historically famous renowned scholars but also these lesser known and a few who have simply left behind a valuable piece of advice to their nearest and dearest. **UK RRP: £5.00**

Ask a Mufti (3 volumes)

Muslims in every generation have confronted different kinds of challenges. In-spite of that, Islām produced such luminary Ulamā who confronted and re-sponded to the challenges of their time to guide the Ummah to the straight path.

"Ask A Mufti" is a comprehensive three volume fatwa book, based on the Hanafi School, covering a wide range of topics related to every aspect of human life such as belief, ritual worship, life after death and contemporary legal topics related to purity, commercial transaction, marriage, divorce, food, cosmetic, laws pertaining to women, Islamic medical ethics and much more.

UK RRP: £30.00

Should I Follow a Madhab?

Taqleed or following one of the four legal schools is not a new phenomenon. Historically, scholars of great calibre and luminaries, each one being a specialist in his own right, were known to have adhered to one of the four legal schools. It is only in the previous century that a minority group emerged advocating a se-vere ban on following one of the four major schools.

This book endeavours to address the topic of Taqleed and elucidates its im-portance and necessity in this day and age. It will also, by the Divine Will of Allāh ﷻ dispel some of the confusion surrounding this topic. **UK RRP: £5.00**

Advice for the Students of Knowledge

Allāh ﷻ describes divine knowledge in the Holy Qur'ān as a 'Light'. Amongst the qualities of light are purity and guidance. The Holy Prophet ﷺ has clearly ex-plained this concept in many blessed Ahādīth and has also taught us many sup-plications in which we ask for beneficial knowledge.

This book is a golden tool for every sincere student of knowledge wishing to mould his/her character and engrain those correct qualities in order to be wor-thy of receiving the great gift of Ilm from Allāh ﷻ. **UK RRP: £3.00**

Stories for Children

"Stories for Children" - is a wonderful gift presented to the readers personally, by the author himself, especially with the young children in mind. The stories are based on moral and ethical values, which the reader will enjoy sharing with their peers, friends, families and loved ones. The aim is to present to the children stories and incidents which contain moral lessons, in order to reform and correct their lives, according to the Holy Qur'ān and Sunnah.

UK RRP: £5.00

Pearls from My Shaykh

This book in your hands contains a collection of pearls and inspirational accounts of the Holy Prophet ﷺ, his noble Companions, pious predecessors and some personal accounts and sayings of our well-known contemporary scholar and spiritual guide, Shaykh Mufti Saiful Islām Sāhib. Each anecdote and narrative of the pious predecessors have been written in the way that was narrated by Mufti Saiful Islām Sāhib in his discourses, drawing the specific lessons he intended from telling the story. The accounts from the life of the Shaykh has been compiled by a particular student based on their own experience and personal observation. **UK RRP: £5.00**

Paradise & Hell

This book is a collection of detailed explanation of Paradise and Hell including the state and conditions of its inhabitants. All the details have been taken from various reliable sources. The purpose of its compilation is for the reader to contemplate and appreciate the innumerable favours, rewards, comfort and unlimited luxuries of Paradise and at the same time take heed from the punishment of Hell. Shaykh Mufti Saiful Islām Sāhib has presented this book in a unique format by including the Tafseer and virtues of Sūrah Ar-Rahmān. **UK RRP: £5.00**

Prayers for Forgiveness

Prayers for Forgiveness' is a short compilation of Du'ās in Arabic, with English translation and transliteration. This book can be studied after 'Du'ā for Beginners' or as a separate book. It includes twenty more Du'ās which have not been mentioned in the previous Du'ā book. It also includes a section of Du'ās from the Holy Qur'ān and a section from the Ahādīth. The book concludes with a section mentioning the Ninety-Nine Names of Allāh ﷻ with its translation and transliteration. **UK RRP: £3.00**

Scattered Pearls

This book is a collection of scattered pearls taken from books, magazines, emails and WhatsApp messages. These pearls will hopefully increase our knowledge, wisdom and make us realise the purpose of life. In this book, Mufti Sāhib has included messages sent to him from scholars, friends and colleagues which will be beneficial and interesting for our readers Inshā-Allāh. **UK RRP: £4.00**

Poems of Wisdom

This book is a collection of poems from those who contributed to the Al-Mumin Magazine in the poems section. The Hadeeth mentions "Indeed some form of poems are full of wisdom." The themes of each poem vary between, wittiness, thought provocation, moral lessons, emotional to name but a few. The readers will benefit from this immensely and make you ponder over the outlook of life in general.

UK RRP: £4.00

Horrors of Judgement Day

This book is a detailed and informative commentary of the first three Sūrahs of the last Juz namely; Sūrah Naba, Sūrah Nāzi'āt and Sūrah Abasa. These Sūrahs vividly depict the horrific events and scenes of the Great Day in order to warn mankind the end of this world. These Sūrahs are an essential reminder for us all to instil the fear and concern of the Day of Judgement and to detach ourselves from the worldly pleasures. Reading this book allows us to attain the true realization of this world and provides essential advices of how to gain eternal salvation in the Hereafter.

RRP: £5:00

Spiritual Heart

It is necessary that Muslims always strive to better themselves at all times and to free themselves from the destructive maladies. This book focusses on three main spiritual maladies; pride, anger and evil gazes. It explains its root causes and offers some spiritual cures. Many examples from the lives of the pious predecessors are used for inspiration and encouragement for controlling the above three maladies. It is hoped that the purification process of the heart becomes easy once the underlying roots of the above maladies are clearly understood. **UK RRP: £5:00**

Hajj & Umrah for Beginners

This book is a step by step guide on Hajj and Umrah for absolute beginners. Many other additional important rulings (Masāil) have been included that will Insha-Allāh prove very useful for our readers. The book also includes some etiquettes of visiting (Ziyārat) of the Holy Prophet's ﷺ blessed Masjid and his Holy Grave.

UK RRP £3:00

Advice for the Spiritual Travellers

This book contains essential guidelines for a spiritual Murīd to gain some familiarity of the science of Tasawwuf. It explains the meaning and aims of Tasawwuf, some understanding around the concept of the soul, and general guidelines for a spiritual Murīd. This is highly recommended book and it is hoped that it gains wider readership among those Murīds who are basically new to the science of Tasawwuf.

UK RRP £3:00

Don't Worry Be Happy

This book is a compilation of sayings and earnest pieces of advice that have been gathered directly from my respected teacher Shaykh Mufti Saiful Islām Sāhib. The book consists of many valuable enlightenments including how to deal with challenges of life, promoting unity, practicing good manners, being optimistic and many other valuable advices. Our respected Shaykh has gathered this Naseehah from meditating, contemplating, analysing and searching for the gems within Qur'anic verses, Ahādeeth and teachings of our Pious Predecessors. **UK RRP £1:00**

Kanzul Bāri

Kanzul Bāri provides a detailed commentary of the Ahādeeth contained in Saheeh al-Bukhāri. The commentary includes Imām Bukhāri's ﷺ biography, the status of his book, spiritual advice, inspirational accounts along with academic discussions related to Fiqh, its application and differences of opinion. Moreover, it answers objections arising in one's mind about certain Ahādeeth. Inquisitive students of Hadeeth will find this commentary a very useful reference book in the final year of their Ālim course for gaining a deeper understanding of the science of Hadeeth. **UK RRP: £15.00**

How to Become a Friend of Allāh ﷺ

The friends of Allāh ﷺ have been described in detail in the Holy Qur'ān and Āhadeeth. This book endeavours its readers to help create a bond with Allāh ﷺ in attaining His friendship as He is the sole Creator of all material and immaterial things. It is only through Allāh's ﷺ friendship, an individual will achieve happiness in this life and the Hereafter, hence eliminate worries, sadness, depression, anxiety and misery of this world. **UK RRP:**

Gems & Jewels

This book contains a selection of articles which have been gathered for the benefit of the readers covering a variety of topics on various aspects of daily life. It offers precious advice and anecdotes that contain moral lessons. The advice captivates its readers and will extend the narrowness of their thoughts to deep reflection, wisdom and appreciation of the purpose of our existence. **UK RRP: £4.00**

End of Time

This book is a comprehensive explanation of the three Sūrahs of Juzz Amma; Sūrah Takweer, Sūrah Infitār and Sūrah Mutaffifeen. This book is a continuation from the previous book of the same author, 'Horrors of Judgement Day'. The three Sūrahs vividly sketch out the scene of the Day of Judgement and describe the state of both the inmates of Jannah and Jahannam. Mufti Saiful Islām Sāhib provides an easy but comprehensive commentary of the three Sūrahs facilitating its understanding for the readers whilst capturing the horrific scene of the ending of the world and the conditions of mankind on that horrific Day. **UK RRP: £5.00**

Andalus (modern day Spain), the long lost history, was once a country that produced many great calibre of Muslim scholars comprising of Mufassirūn, Muhaddithūn, Fuqahā, judges, scientists, philosophers, surgeons, to name but a few. The Muslims conquered Andalus in 711 AD and ruled over it for eight-hundred years. This was known as the era of Muslim glory. Many non-Muslim Europeans during that time travelled to Spain to study under Muslim scholars. The remanences of the Muslim rule in Spain are manifested through their universities, magnificent palaces and Masājid carved with Arabic writings, standing even until today. In this book, Shaykh Mufti Saiful Islām shares some of his valuable experiences he witnessed during his journey to Spain. **UK RRP: £3.00**

Ideal Youth

This book contains articles gathered from various social media avenues; magazines, emails, WhatsApp and telegram messages that provide useful tips of advice for those who have the zeal to learn and consider changing their negative habits and behavior and become better Muslims to set a positive trend for the next generation. **UK RRP:£4:00**

Ideal Teacher

This book contains abundance of precious advices for the Ulamā who are in the teaching profession. It serves to present Islamic ethical principles of teaching and to remind every teacher of their moral duties towards their students. This book will Inshā-Allāh prove to be beneficial for newly graduates and scholars wanting to utilize their knowledge through teaching. **UK RRP:£4:00**

Ideal Student

This book is a guide for all students of knowledge in achieving the excellent qualities of becoming an ideal student. It contains precious advices, anecdotes of our pious predecessors and tips in developing good morals as a student. Good morals is vital for seeking knowledge. A must for all students if they want to develop their Islamic Knowledge. **UK RRP:£4:00**

Ideal Parents

This book contains a wealth of knowledge in achieving the qualities of becoming ideal parents. It contains precious advices, anecdotes of our pious predecessors and tips in developing good parenthood skills. Good morals is vital for seeking knowledge. A must for all parents . **UK RRP:£4:00**

Ideal Couple

This book is a compilation of inspiring stories and articles containing useful tips and life skills for every couple. Marriage life is a big responsibility and success in marriage is only possible if the couple know what it means to be an ideal couple. **UK RRP:£4:00**

Ideal Role Model

This book is a compilation of sayings and accounts of our pious predecessors. The purpose of this book is so we can learn from our pious predecessors the purpose of this life and how to attain closer to the Creator. Those people who inspires us attaining closeness to our Creator are our true role models. A must everyone to read. **UK RRP:£4:00**

Bangladesh– A Land of Natural Beauty

This book is a compilation of our respected Shaykh's journeys to Bangladesh including visits to famous Madāris and Masājid around the country. The Shaykh shares some of his thought provoking experiences and his personal visits with great scholars in Bangladesh. **UK RRP: £4.00**

Pearls from the Quran

This series begins with the small Sūrahs from 30th Juzz initially, unravelling its heavenly gems, precious advices and anecdotes worthy of personal reflection. It will most definitely benefit both those new to as well as advanced students of the science of Tafsīr. The purpose is to make it easily accessible for the general public in understanding the meaning of the Holy Qur'ān. **UK RRP:**